SCARED!

HAUNTING URBAN LEGENDS

BY MEGAN COOLEY PETERSON

Consultant:
Simon J. Bronner
Distinguished Professor of American Studies and Folklore
Chair, American Studies Program
Pennsylvania State University

CAPSTONE PRESS
a capstone imprint

Snap Books are published by Capstone Press,
1710 Roe Crest Drive, North Mankato, Minnesota 56003
www.capstonepub.com

Library of Congress Cataloging-in-Publication Data
Peterson, Megan Cooley.
Haunting urban legends / by Megan Cooley Peterson.
    pages cm. — (Snap. Scared.)
Includes bibliographical references and index.
Summary: "Spooky retellings of well-known urban legends"—Provided
by publisher.
ISBN 978-1-4296-9983-9 (library binding)
ISBN 978-1-4765-3561-6 (ebook PDF)
1. Urban folklore. I. Title.
GR78.P47 2014
398.2—dc23   2013005399

Editorial Credits
Mari Bolte, editor; Ashlee Suker, designer; Wanda Winch, media researcher;
Charmaine Whitman, production specialist

Photo Credits
BJ Winslow, cover, 8 (hook); Capstone Studio: Karon Dubke, 10, 29; Shutterstock:
Ann Cantelow, 7, Artem Furman, 26, Brian A. Jackson, 9, chalabala, 30, Henrik Larsson,
17 (right), Jandrie Lombard, 4, kavram, 16, keren-seg, 2, 6, 15, 24, 28, Kzenon, 14,
La Vieja Sirena, 21, Ilaszlo, cover 1 (dark road), Marko Bradic, 19 (door), Otokimus, 3,
Peter Dedeurwaerder, 22, posztos, 25, Potapov Alexander, 27 (spiders), prudkov, 4–5
(background), Reinhold Leitner, 18-19 (background), Roger costa morera, 18 (dog),
spirit of America, 12

Design Elements
Shutterstock: Athos Boncompagni Illustratore, cover splatters, basel 101658, tree
branch silhouette, C. Salisbury, winter tree frame, cluckva, stone wall design, David M.
Schrader, brush frame, Emelyanov, fractal pattern, foxie, brush stroke photo captions,
grivet, beige texture, happykanppy, black water color, HiSunnySky, red grunge frame,
Igor Shikov, blue frame, javarman, tree frame, cloud background, kanate, olive water
color, Leksus Tuss, red, green scratch texture, Massimo Saivezzo, grunge floral, yel-
low, mcherevan, chandelier, NinaMalyna, purple frame, optimarc, line brush texture,
pashabo, grunge red border, PeterPhoto123, smoke, Pixel 4 Images, trees section, branch
design, Reinhold Leitner, blue smudge frame, Theeradech Sanin, distressed wood frame

Printed in the United States of America in North Mankato, Minnesota.
122013   007904R

Table of Contents

4

Introduction

Too Scary to Be True

It's late at night. You're at a slumber party. As the wind howls outside, you snuggle deeper into your sleeping bag. One of your friends starts telling a spooky story. She holds a flashlight under her chin as she tells her tale. The story seems too scary to be true. But your friend says it really happened to a friend of someone she knows. The hairs on the back of your neck stand up. Maybe the story is true. Maybe it could happen to you.

An urban legend is a strange and often scary story told as if it really happened. It's passed on by word of mouth and on the Internet. Despite the name, urban legends are told throughout the world, in both urban and rural areas. They are sometimes called "belief legends." Urban legends often take common fears, such as babysitting at night or driving in the dark, and twist them into terrifying tales. These stories scare us because they could happen. They also warn us by telling us what not to do.

The urban legends in this book are some of the most bizarre stories ever told. Are you feeling brave?

Then turn the page if you dare.

Chapter One

On the Road

The Hook

Two sisters drove down an empty gravel road. Moonlight filtered through the trees to guide their path. They were going on their summer camping trip. One sister was adventurous. She couldn't wait to tell scary stories by the fire. The other sister was shy. She hated the dark and wished she were curled up at home with a good book.

They drove deep into the woods to their campsite. The shy sister jumped when her cell phone beeped. It was a text from a friend. It was a chilling message. A patient had just escaped from a nearby mental institution. The man had a hook in place of his right hand. He was last spotted near their campsite.

The "man with a hook" legend has been told since the 1950s.

"We should go home," the shy sister said as she locked the car doors. "What if he's out there?"

"You watch too much TV. Nothing bad will happen to us."

Suddenly a high-pitched squeak cut through the silence. It sounded as if a piece of metal were being dragged against the car. "Did you hear that?" the shy sister asked. "Let's go!"

Sighing, the adventurous sister sped out of the woods. She was furious with her sister for ruining their trip.

When they got home, she climbed out of the car and slammed her door shut. "Are you happy?" she asked.

But her sister didn't answer. Instead she let out a bloodcurdling scream. The adventurous sister ran around to the passenger's side of the car. Hanging from one of the door handles was a bloody hook.

The Stolen Kidney

A traveling salesman was driving alone late one night. He was hungry and tired and decided to stop at the next hotel.

After he checked in, he went to the hotel restaurant. He ordered a cheeseburger and a diet soda. The man got his cheeseburger, but the waitress apologized and said they were out of diet soda. Another man sat a few tables away from the salesman. He offered his soda cup to the man. "Would you like mine?" he asked. "The waitress just brought it. I haven't taken a drink from it yet."

The salesman thanked the stranger and took the soda. As he sipped, he grew very sleepy and closed his eyes for a moment.

He awoke in a bathtub filled with ice. Sitting on a table next to the tub was a phone. A note taped to the phone said, "Call 911." The salesman called the police and explained where he was. The operator asked the salesman if he had a large incision along the side of his body.

The salesman plunged his hand into the sharp pieces of ice. He felt along his side until his fingers touched a long line of stitches. His teeth chattered when he spoke. "Y-yes. I can feel a long cut."

"Stay where you are," the operator said. "I've already sent an ambulance."

"W-what's wrong with me?" the man asked.

"Try not to panic, sir, but someone has stolen one of your kidneys."

Traveler Beware!

The missing kidney story has been told since the late 1980s. But is it true? In 2000 the National Kidney Foundation sent out a message. They asked anyone who had had their kidney illegally removed to contact them. So far, nobody has.

The Attacker in the Backseat

A girl hurried across a damp road and climbed inside her car. She had stayed too late at a friend's house studying, and now it was dark outside. Driving at night made the girl nervous. She yanked on her seatbelt and checked her mirrors. But there was one thing she had forgotten to check before she left—the gas gauge. The needle pointed at empty.

The girl stopped at the nearest gas station. One of the building's windows had been smashed, and the pumps were rusted over.

The only other customer was a man filling up his truck. He grinned at her. The girl turned away and started the gas pump.

"Good evening," the man said.

She craned her head over her shoulder, smiled weakly, and turned back toward her car.

"Can I talk to you?" the man asked. "It'll only take a minute."

"Why?"

"Come over here, and I'll tell you."

The girl hauled the nozzle out of her car and clawed for her receipt. "I don't think so," she said as she hurled herself into the car and sped away. She glanced in her rearview mirror just in time to see the truck come to life. Its headlights bounced up and down as it tore out of the gas station.

When the girl turned left, the truck made the exact same turn. She pushed harder on the gas pedal. The truck also picked up speed. Then the man flashed his lights and honked his horn.

"What do you want?" the girl screamed, speeding down an unfamiliar street. The truck kept pace behind her. Finally her house appeared up ahead. She pulled into the driveway, slammed on the brakes, and jumped out of the car.

In every version of this story, the driver is female. The person who warns her and the attacker are always male.

But it was too late. The man parked the truck and was only steps behind her.

"Leave me alone!" she yelled. The man stopped and gave her a puzzled look. Then he opened the back door of her car. Inside was a bleeding man holding a knife. He had fallen to the car floor during the chase and accidentally stabbed himself.

Chapter Two

Inside the House

Don't Go Upstairs

Rain splattered against the main lodge of a summer camp nestled deep in the woods. All of the campers were away on an overnight trip, except for one counselor and two sick children.

The counselor tucked the children in for the night. She shut the bedroom door behind her and walked down a large staircase made of logs. When a crack of thunder rattled the lodge, she let out a scream.

"Quit being such a baby," she thought. She curled up on a couch and tried to read a book. Flames crackled in the stone fireplace. She jumped when the phone rang. "Hello?" she asked.

In some versions of the babysitter urban legend, there is no man upstairs. The calls are made by the children.

She heard a man's voice. "Have you checked on the children? At midnight I'm going to get them, and then I'm going to get you!"

The girl figured it was a prank call and hung up. She had just finished making popcorn when the phone rang again.

"Better come upstairs and check on the children. At midnight I'm going to get them, and then I'm going to get you!" The voice was the same as before.

"This isn't funny!" she said, slamming down the phone.

She turned her back when the phone rang a third time.

"It's almost midnight," the man said. "Last chance!"

Now the girl was afraid. Maybe it wasn't a prank. She thought about calling the other counselors. Instead she dialed the police. The operator told her they would trace the call.

The man called again a few minutes later. "What do you want?" the girl asked. The man laughed and hung up.

When the phone rang again, she was afraid to answer it. Her hand trembled. "Hello?" she whispered.

It was the police. "We've traced the call. It's coming from a cell phone inside the lodge. Get out now."

"But what about the children? They're alone upstairs!"

"Get out now," the police officer repeated. "We're on our way. And whatever you do, don't go upstairs."

Just as the counselor put down the phone, a shadowy figure moved on the staircase. It was a man holding a large butcher knife. "It's midnight," he cackled.

The girl screamed and ran into the forest. She hid behind an oak tree as the rain pelted her skin. Soon two police cars pulled up, and the officers arrested the man. They found the children upstairs, still asleep in their beds.

The Choking Dog

A woman lifted a heavy bag of groceries from her car and carried it into her house. "Buddy!" she called out. Her large dog, Buddy, usually greeted her the moment she came home. "Buddy?"

"That's odd," the woman thought. She went from room to room, looking for Buddy. She found him lying on her bedroom floor, gasping for air. The woman scooped Buddy into her arms and drove him to the veterinarian.

"Help! I think my dog is choking!"

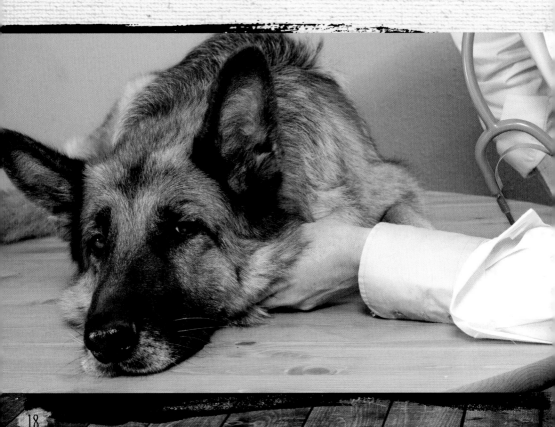

The vet performed a quick exam. Buddy would need surgery to locate the cause of his problem. "It might take a couple of hours," the vet said. "I'll call you when I'm finished."

The woman was upset but drove home to wait for the vet's call. She had just pulled into the driveway when her cell phone rang. It was the vet. "Don't go in the house! Don't ask any questions. I've already called the police."

When the police arrived, an officer explained what happened. During surgery the vet found a very gruesome surprise lodged in Buddy's throat—three human fingers. Passed out in the woman's bedroom closet lay a burglar. The police arrested the burglar, and Buddy returned home a hero.

The Roommate

It was the week before Christmas vacation. Two college roommates were the only girls left in their dormitory. Late one night, one of the girls went downstairs for a snack. The other girl stayed in the room and locked the door. She searched for a movie to watch. She had just turned on the TV when she heard a sound in the hallway.

Thump.

She looked at the clock that hung next to the window. Her roommate had been gone for nearly a half hour. "Hello?" she called.

Thump.

"Who's out there?" The roommates had a special knock to let the other know to let them in. What if it wasn't her roommate in the hall?

Scratch. Scratch. Scratch.

The girl covered her ears as the sounds from the hallway grew louder. She eventually fell asleep.

The next morning, she was afraid to open the door. She pulled open the window and shouted down to the mailman walking by.

The mailman told her he would check the hallway.

He disappeared for a moment and then returned. "Everything's

all right," he told the girl. "Just don't leave your room."

But the girl didn't listen. She turned the lock and pulled

open the door. Her dead roommate was right outside.

Her fingernails had been worn down to bloody stumps,

and there were long scratches in the door.

The Creepy Statue

A girl arrived at her first babysitting job after dark. The large house was covered in peeling paint. One of the windows was broken. She took a deep breath and knocked on the front door. The parents answered and told her the children were already asleep upstairs.

"Our home is quite large, and you might get lost," the woman said. "Please just stay in the living room." They gave the girl their cell phone number and left.

The girl settled on the couch to do some homework. But she couldn't stop staring at a large clown statue in the corner of the room. She tried to ignore it, but its lopsided smile and bright, red wig gave her the creeps. She wanted to move to a different room but remembered the woman's instructions. The babysitter called the parents and asked if she could throw a blanket over the statue.

"Get the children and leave the house," the parents said. "We'll call the police."

The babysitter found the children and waited in the front yard. She was confused when the police arrived and carried the clown statue out of the house. Only it wasn't a statue at all. It was a man dressed up as a clown.

Beauty and the Beast

The Deadly Tan

For the safety of their customers, tanning salons limit the amount of time a person can tan. Unfortunately for one girl, she chose not to listen.

It was a few days before the prom. The girl had the perfect dress. She slipped it on and stood in front of her bedroom mirror. She decided she looked too pale. She drove straight to the nearest tanning salon. After her session she asked if she could book another appointment for later that same day. The woman behind the counter explained that she could not tan for more than 30 minutes each day.

The girl stormed out of the salon. At this pace she would never be tan in time for the dance. Then she had an idea. For the next few days, she drove to every salon in town and tanned for hours each day. Her skin turned red and raw, but she knew she would look amazing in her prom dress.

When the night of the dance arrived, the girl could barely find the strength to put on her gown. Her vision dimmed as she walked downstairs to meet her date. "Do you smell that?" her date asked. "It smells like cooked meat."

The girl tried to answer. Instead she fell into a heap on the floor. Smoke poured out from her eyes and mouth. Too many tanning sessions had boiled her from the inside out.

An Outfit to Die For

A girl received a party invitation from one of the most popular students in school. Wanting to look her best, she searched the Internet for something new to wear. She bought an expensive-looking sweater on a discount website.

At the party the girl received many compliments on her new sweater. She had fun playing games and talking with her friends. But as the party wore on, she began to feel strange. Sweat dripped down her face. She had trouble breathing. Finally she went to get some fresh air. She never returned.

Her friends found her collapsed outside and called an ambulance. But it was too late. The girl's death remained a mystery until the medical examiner found a deadly amount of formaldehyde in her body. The police discovered the sweater had previously belonged to a corpse. The toxic chemicals from the dead body had soaked into the sweater's fabric—and into the sweater's new owner.

The Bite

A girl had just returned from a family vacation to Florida and brought home an ugly and unwanted souvenir—a large pimple. The new school year was only a few days away.

She didn't want to be seen with such a hideous blemish.

The girl tried everything to get rid of the mark. She washed her face several times a day. She applied creams and lotions. But the bump only grew larger and more painful. Once she even thought she saw the pimple move. She climbed into bed the night before school, dreading the next day.

In the dead of night, a sharp, stabbing pain shot through her pimple. She raced into her bathroom and squeezed the zit until it popped. Only it wasn't pus that oozed from the wound. Hundreds of tiny, black spiders crawled out from the bump and scurried all over her face.

Chapter Four

Beyond the Grave

The Ghostly Visitor

A doctor arrived home from a long day at the hospital. A blizzard raged outside. He sat down to watch TV when he heard three sharp knocks on his front door. A young girl dressed in a red coat stood outside.

"Please help me," she said. "My mother is very sick. We have to hurry."

The doctor grabbed his medical bag and put on his warmest coat. He followed the girl out into the storm. They soon arrived at a small house. The girl led the doctor to a room at the end of a dark hall. "My mother is in there," she said, pointing to the door. "Please help her."

The doctor nodded and entered the room. A woman lay

in the bed. Light from a single candle danced around the

room. The doctor examined the woman. "It's a good thing your

daughter came to me when she did," he said.

The woman crinkled her brow. "My daughter? It can't be.

She died a month ago."

"But I just spoke with her. She's wearing a red coat."

The woman slowly raised her arm and pointed at the closet.

When the doctor opened the door, there was the girl's red coat,

speckled with fresh snow.

Repost ... Or Else

Late one night a boy sat in front of his computer, surfing the Internet. A tree swayed in the roaring wind. The boy jumped as the branches scratched against the house.

Only it wasn't a tree that frightened the boy. It was the story he found online. The boy leaned in close to the screen as he read the chilling tale. A few years ago, a girl stood outside the school with her friends during a fire drill. She fell down a manhole and into the sewer. By the time the police arrived, it was too late. The fall had killed the girl.

A shudder ran up the boy's spine as he read the ending of the story. The girl's ghost returned and said her friends pushed her into the sewer—on purpose. And now anyone who didn't repost her story would meet the same deadly end.

The boy was about to repost the story when the power went out. He forgot to repost the girl's story.

The boy was never seen alive again. Days later the police found his body in the sewer.

Internet Legends

The "girl pushed down a storm drain" story is a worldwide urban legend. In October 2011 it was the most-searched Internet story in the Philippines. E-mail urban legends with warnings to repost or forward chain letters ("or else") have been around for decades. They have become even more common with the help of social media sites such as Facebook and Twitter.

READ MORE

Lynette, Rachel. *Urban Legends.* Mysterious Encounters. Detroit: Kidhaven Press, 2008.

O'Shei, Tim. *Creepy Urban Legends.* Scary Stories. Mankato, Minn.: Capstone Press, 2011.

Stewart, Gail B. *Urban Legends.* The Mysterious & Unknown. San Diego, Calif.: Reference Point Books, 2012.

INTERNET SITES

FactHound offers a safe, fun way to find Internet sites related to this book. All of the sites on FactHound have been researched by our staff.

Here's all you do:

Visit *www.facthound.com*

Type in this code: 9781429699839

 Check out projects, games and lots more at **www.capstonekids.com**

OTHER TITLES IN THIS SET: